STARTING DESIGN & TECHNOLOGY

BUSINESS AND ENTERPRISE

BILL NICHOLL AND PETER STENSEL

Series editor: John Cave

CASSELL

Cassell
Villiers House, 41/47 Strand, London WC2N 5JE, England

First published 1992

British Library Cataloguing-in-Publication Data
Nicholl, Bill, *1966–*
  Business and enterprise. – (Starting design and technology)
  I. Title II. Stensel, Peter, *1965–*
  338.7

ISBN 0–304–32371–3

Typeset by Fakenham Photosetting Limited, Fakenham,
Norfolk

Printed and bound in Great Britain by
Courier International Ltd., East Kilbride

Contents

Introduction   5

1 Business Enterprise   6
What Is a Business?   6
Types of Industries   7
What Is Involved in Running a Business?   8
The Development of a Business:
   Part 1   10
   Part 2   12
   Part 3   14
   Part 4   16

2 Marketing—an Introduction   18
Markets and Marketing   18
Market Research   20
The Marketing Mix   24
The Business Plan   31
The Business Environment   32

3 Design for Manufacture   34
The Pizza Parlour   34
The Pizza Parlour Recipe   35

Types of Production   37
Consumer Requirements   38
Packaging the Pizza   40
Information Design   42
Desktop Publishing   43
Nutrition Information   44
Running the Parlour   46

4 Marketing and the Environment   48
What Is the Environment?   48
Damaging the Environment   50
Consumers and the Environment   52
Government and the Environment   53
Design and the Environment   54
Marketing, Design and the Environment   55
Recycling   56
Reusing   57

Mini-Dictionary   58

Index   62

Introduction

Imagine what life would be like without farms and mines or without products such as washing machines and telephones. Where would we be without the services of banks, garages or the transport system? It's hard to imagine, isn't it? These products and services help to improve the quality of our lives.

Where do we begin, though, when we want to produce a new product or service? There is more to it than just having the idea. This book will help uncover and explain the mysteries of the business world.

Section 1 (Business Enterprise) examines what a business is and gives examples of different types. It looks at what is involved in running a business and suggests how a new one might develop.

Section 2 is all about marketing. It covers topics such as market research and the four ingredients that make up the marketing mix.

The third section covers design for manufacture and is based around a small business called The Pizza Parlour.

The final section (Marketing and the Environment) brings the world of business and enterprise up to date, covering environmental issues and shows how they are becoming big business!

Read the four sections carefully, one after the other. There are regular tasks for you to do and a Mini-Dictionary at the back of this book will help you to understand any new words or terms you come across.

Fact File

- The amount of money in circulation in Britain is enough to create a 300-kilometre-high pile of £5 notes!

- Some tribes in East Africa have used goats as a form of money but problems of disease and storage have made them unsuitable. Shells, axes, tea and 3-metre-wide boulders have been used in other cultures!

1 Business Enterprise

What Is a Business?

Think about the last time you went to a shopping centre. What different types of shops were there? You may, for example, have seen a butcher's, a newsagent's, a greengrocer's or a shoe shop. Make a list of as many different kinds of shops as you can think of.

Shops are one type of business which supply **products** we need, such as food, clothes, books and furniture. Factories are another kind of business. They make the products which are sold in the shops. Some are large with a long **production line**, such as a car manufacturer's. Others may be small and run from home, such as a dressmaker's.

Other types of business sell a **service** rather than an actual product. Hairdressers, car repair garages and dry cleaners, for example, would be included in this group. It is the time and skill for which we pay rather than the product.

Some businesses are small and run by one or two people only, such as a market stall. Others may be much bigger with several departments and a large number of staff.

Below is a list of several different kinds of business.

Department store	**Hardware shop**	**Bank**
Baker	**Garage**	**Travel agent**
Butcher	**Fish shop**	**Blacksmith**
Hairdresser	**Window cleaner**	**Greengrocer**
Coal mine	**Printer**	**Solicitor**
Brewery	**Estate agent**	**Transport**
Optician	**Milkman**	**Farming**
School	**Photographer**	**Hotel**
Theme park	**Forestry**	**Furniture**
Textile factory	**Jeweller**	**maker**

Although they are all very different from each other, all businesses fall into one of three groups.

Fact File

One of the first uses of mass production in the business world was made by Henry Ford in the USA. In 1914 he set up a moving assembly line to produce a motor car called the Model T, which became very popular. The Ford company is still producing cars today.

Types of Industries

Primary industries

Primary industries are those which extract things normally provided by nature; they include, for example, mining, fishing and farming. They may produce **raw materials** such as oil, iron or coal, which are used to make other products. Alternatively, they may produce final products such as fish or fruit.

Secondary industries

Secondary industries make products. They **manufacture** them, using raw materials and parts from other industries. Many products such as cookers, televisions and cars involve several stages of production. Secondary industries are also known as manufacturing and construction industries.

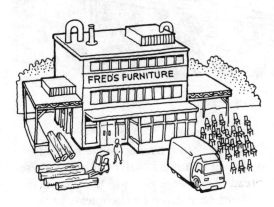

Tertiary industries

Tertiary industries are those such as banks, window cleaners and lawyers which provide a service and not physical goods. Tertiary industries are also called service industries and have become very important in recent years. Other examples include transport, insurance, leisure centres and places of entertainment such as cinemas.

Task

Study the list of businesses on the opposite page. Try to divide the list into three groups under the headings of Primary, Secondary and Tertiary industries. Can you think of any other businesses which could be added to these groups?

Business Enterprise

What Is Involved in Running a Business?

However small or large a business is, a great deal of organization and planning must take place if things are to run smoothly. A lot more is involved in a bakery, for example, than simply baking the bread. Ingredients have to be ordered from various suppliers and stored in a suitable place. Other materials such as bags, boxes and cleaning materials must also be ordered. The equipment such as the ovens, freezers and slicing machines must be kept in good working order if the business is to succeed.

There are many duties other than baking the bread. Most bakers will produce buns, doughnuts and tarts, also cakes, perhaps made to order for birthdays or weddings. Packaging and distribution must be organized, bills must be paid and advertisements placed in local papers.

Labour force

Several people may be employed, including a baker to bake the bread, a chef to make the cakes and a cleaner to clean the equipment and the premises. Some of the jobs will need more skill than others but all of the workers will rely on each other: each person must carry out his or her own duties. The people who work for a business are known as the **labour force**. Large companies can have a labour force of thousands of people.

Fact File

- The Romans liked bread. About 258 bakeries were trading in Rome by 100 BC. Later, a school for bakers was set up by the emperor Trajan.

- Bread was often used to make plates for medieval banquets. After the feast, these bread plates were given to the poor if they had not been eaten by the guests.

What Is Involved in Running a Business?

Like all businesses, the bakery will have a lot of things to pay for. These are called its **costs**. The baker and other staff must be paid and there will be bills for heating, lighting and telephone calls. Other costs will include rates, insurance and the purchase of materials. It will, therefore, be necessary to sell a lot of bread and cakes to make enough money to pay the bills. The money which is left after all the bills have been paid is called the **profit**.

People may set up a new business for various reasons. Some may aim to make as much money as they can. These would be called commercial businesses. However, the wish for a large profit is not always the main reason for setting up a new business. For many people, it is the challenge and the freedom of working for themselves which is more important. They may be prepared to earn less so long as they are working at something they enjoy.

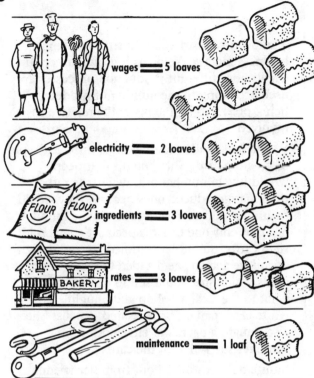

A comparison of costs for the bakery, showing relatively how many loaves of bread must be sold in order to cover various costs.

Task

One of the most important ways of attracting business for a company is through **advertising**. The bakery will advertise its service of baking cakes for special occasions such as birthdays and weddings. What do you think should be included in such an advert for a local paper? How might it be designed to stand out from other adverts in the paper?

How much space do you think would be needed to make an effective advertisement? Try to find out what your local newspaper charges for different amounts of advertising space and make a guess as to how much space a small bakery might be able to afford. After considering these questions, design a suitable advertisement for the bakery.

Business Enterprise

The Development of a Business: Part 1

This section looks at how a small design business might develop as it grows larger. It shows how different production processes are used according to the number of products being produced and looks at the relative costs involved.

Sunita had an idea for making a different type of greeting card. She thought that people would like to buy hand-drawn cards rather than mass-produced ones because they would be unique and therefore special. She found out that only one or two specialist shops sold such cards. Sunita had studied art and design at college and so she decided to make some cards which she would sell to friends. She went to the local art shop and bought some white card, paints, brushes and pencils. She also bought a packet of envelopes from a stationer's to sell with the cards.

Sunita decided to find out from her friends what sort of cards they liked. She made a questionnaire which her friends filled in and from the answers to this Sunita was able to see what might be popular. She worked in the evenings painting the cards. She produced about three cards each night and used a stencil to write a simple message inside each one. Sunita worked out that she needed to sell at least six cards to cover the cost of the materials which she had bought.

Task

Questionnaires can be very useful for finding out what people like and dislike. What sort of questions do you think Sunita might have asked in her questionnaire? Think about the way cards can vary in shape and size. Some are funny, others serious. Some have long messages inside, others have no message at all. Cards can be plain, abstract, musical and even have a pop-up mechanism.

How might the information gained from the questionnaire have been recorded? For people to write out their thoughts in full would be very time-consuming. An alternative might be to suggest several answers for each question. People would then simply tick the answer with which they agreed.

Your task is to design and produce a questionnaire to find out what sort of cards people like and dislike. Use the questionnaire to find out how choices differ, for example, between young and old people, males and females and different cultures.

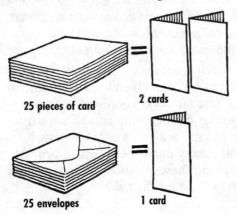

25 pieces of card = 2 cards

25 envelopes = 1 card

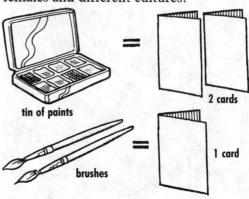

tin of paints = 2 cards

brushes = 1 card

The Development of a Business: Part 1

By the end of the first week Sunita had sold ten cards and her friends were asking for more for their friends. As time went on, Sunita realized that people really liked her cards. She wondered how she could reduce the time it took to make each one so that she produced more each evening. She tried various methods including potato printing, using stencils, rubber stamps and wax. She found that she was now able to produce three times as many cards each week. She stored them in cardboard boxes in her wardrobe and put an advertisement in the window of the local newsagent. At the weekends, Sunita sold her cards from door to door at homes in the neighbourhood. She used her bicycle as transport, which had a detachable bag to hold the cards.

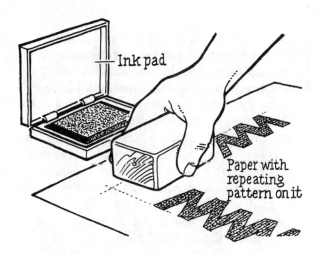

Rubber-stamp printing

One way of reproducing a design is to use a rubber stamp and an ink pad. The stamp is made by drawing the design onto a piece of rubber, such as part of an old inner tube. The design is cut out using a scalpel or scissors and stuck to a flat wooden block with double-sided tape.

To use the stamp it is first wetted on an ink pad and then stamped onto a material such as paper or fabric. Ink pads are available in various colours and can be bought from most stationers. Interesting designs can be built up as a tile pattern using a single stamp.

Fact File

Computers are now used to work out the results of large-scale questionnaires. Marks on the paper are read by a beam of light and the position of the mark determines its meaning to the computer. Some of your exam papers will also be marked in a similar way!

Task

Using the rubber-stamp printing method, design a pattern which could be used on an invitation card for a party. The party might be to celebrate a birthday, a religious festival or a wedding anniversary. Your design should reflect the results from your questionnaire. Fifty invitations are required and they should show the date, time and place of the party in clearly written handwriting, typing or printing.

The Development of a Business: Part 2

As time went on, Sunita found that she was spending as much time selling the cards as making them. She decided to ask a friend to join her. This meant that she would have to share the profit, because she had to pay her friend, and so she needed to find a way of increasing her output of cards. Photocopying was one idea. Black and white photocopying was reasonably cheap and therefore added little to the cost of each card. Sunita produced some new designs in black ink which photocopied very well. All she needed to do was to fold the card and it was ready for sale. She spent her time producing the cards while her friend looked after the selling side of the business. Sunita knew that the cards were no longer all originals, but as long as they sold she didn't mind.

They placed an advertisement in the local paper and managed to hire a stall at the market. They invested in a motor bike for transporting the cards and materials. Sunita knew that she now had a lot more to pay out for and would therefore need to sell many more cards to make a profit. She also found she needed more room to work and to store the cards and so she set herself up in the garage. Her parents' car had to live outside!

Many cards were sold at the market but people began to ask for some of her original colour designs. How could she reproduce the coloured cards? To have them printed would work out very expensive for each card unless she had several thousand made.

The main cost in printing is for the time and effort needed to set up and prepare the printing machinery. This cost will be the same no matter how many cards are being made. To work out the cost of making each card, the costs of printing are divided by the number of cards made. This is the **unit cost**. The unit cost is high for a small number of cards because the costs are spread out over a few cards only. For a large number of cards, it would be lower.

Sunita decided that at this stage she could not afford to have the cards printed. She decided, instead, to use a colour photocopier. This, too, was expensive but she found that she could fit two designs on each copy. Although the copies were not as good as the originals, they still sold well. There were two or three regular customers who bought cards from her to sell in their own shops. It was not long before Sunita was selling over a thousand cards per week.

The Development of a Business: Part 2

Photocopying

Photocopying is one of the most widely used methods of copying written words or artwork. Most schools and offices use photocopiers to reproduce letters, information sheets and worksheets for staff or students. There are many different kinds of photocopier available. Most will produce only single-colour copies but some will copy in full colour. Bigger machines can reduce or enlarge and make several copies every second.

Single-colour photocopiers work best when copying a black and white original. This should be remembered when you are producing artwork which will be photocopied. Tones can be made by using black dots or cross-hatching, as shown below.

Many photocopiers will copy onto different types of paper including cartridge paper, coloured paper and thin card.

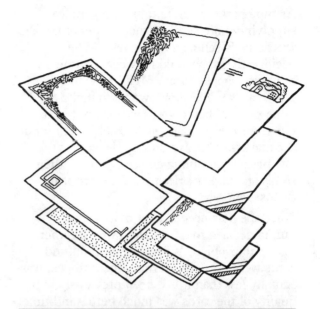

Task

Many stationery shops sell a range of special writing papers and envelopes. These have various designs printed on them, such as drawings of famous people, places or abstract patterns. Sometimes the design covers the page but will be faint enough to allow the writing to show clearly. On other papers, the design might be bold but printed around the edges only.

First look at a few examples, then produce some designs of your own. Your artwork should be designed to be photocopied and will therefore need to be black and white. The paper onto which you are copying, however, may be textured or coloured.

Consider also the design of the envelope. If you use ready-made envelopes you may find it difficult to photocopy a design onto them. Alternatively, you can make your own by photocopying the design onto a single sheet of paper, which is then cut and folded into an envelope.

The Development of a Business: Part 3

As time passed, Sunita found that she was supplying more cards to shop owners than she was actually selling at the market. She decided that she would now concentrate on selling to shops. Sunita would have to sell more cards to the shop owners to make the same profit. Shop owners would not pay as much for the cards as she had sold them for at the market. They would buy the cards at a low price from Sunita and sell them in their shops at a higher price to make a profit for themselves.

Since she now needed a lot more cards, Sunita decided to have them printed rather than photocopied. When several thousand cards were printed at a time, the unit cost was actually less than it had been previously. The quality of the cards was much better and time was saved because the machine folded the cards as well.

However, Sunita worked out that to make a good profit she would need to supply more shops than she already was doing. She placed an advertisement in a national newspaper and had a commercial made for the local radio station.

As more orders came in, Sunita decided to expand to larger premises and take on more staff. She rented a small unit on an industrial estate and bought some second-hand printing machinery. She employed people to help with the printing and packing of the cards and bought a van to distribute the goods. Although her printing costs were reduced, Sunita now had rent to pay on the premises along with the electricity bills and wages.

As a way of increasing business, she started producing posters and postcards as well as greeting cards. She gave her company a name and designed a logo for it. This logo was printed on all the materials the company produced and was painted on the side of the van. To Sunita, this was like putting her signature on everything the company produced. Eventually, she was distributing over 5000 cards and posters each week to stores all over the country.

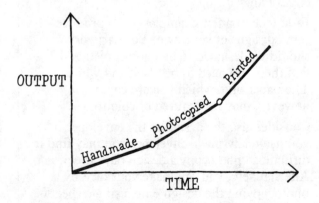

The graph shows how the output has changed during the development of Sunita's business.

The Development of a Business: Part 3

Corporate identity

The reputation of a company can be the most important factor affecting its performance. A company with a good reputation will obviously attract more business than one with a bad reputation. A large company will spend a great deal of money developing its corporate identity to help ensure a good reputation.

Corporate identity is the idea people have of a company—how they see it, both visually and non-visually. The visual part might include such things as:

- Logos
- Headed papers
- Signs
- Packaging
- Promotional material
- Uniforms

The non-visual parts will include such things as the way staff talk to customers and how the company behaves towards the environment.

A range of logos from various companies and organizations.

Fact File

One tree provides enough pulp for about 400 newspapers. Britain would need to cut down a forest as big as Wales each year if all its paper was made from home-grown pulp!

Task

A company's logo is an important part of its corporate identity. It is a symbol to identify the company. The important points of a logo include:

- Visibility—it should always stand out clearly
- It should be interesting to look at
- It should be easy to remember

Remembering these points, think of a name for Sunita's company and design a logo which she could use.

In recent years, people have become more and more concerned about the environment we live in. What do you think Sunita's company could do to build a good reputation for its care for the environment?

Business Enterprise

The Development of a Business: Part 4

Sunita's cards and posters became very popular and the business was making a good profit. However, she found that she was spending so much time organizing the business that little time was left to design new cards. Sunita decided that she would employ someone to manage the business for her so that she could spend more time doing what she enjoyed most—actually designing the cards.

How could Sunita expand her business from here? She was already selling cards and posters all over the country. One option would be to produce a wider range of products, such as stationery or printed fabrics. However, she decided instead to try selling her cards and posters abroad. This meant a much wider advertising campaign, which included European magazines and broadcasting stations. Sunita knew that she would have to be ready for foreign enquiries. She needed people who were fluent in foreign languages to speak on the phone and reply to letters.

Sunita began to plan for the future. She would need a larger factory with better printing machines and more storage space. Its position would have to allow easy distribution both throughout the country and also to ports for overseas markets. She would also need lorries rather than vans to cope with the large number of orders.

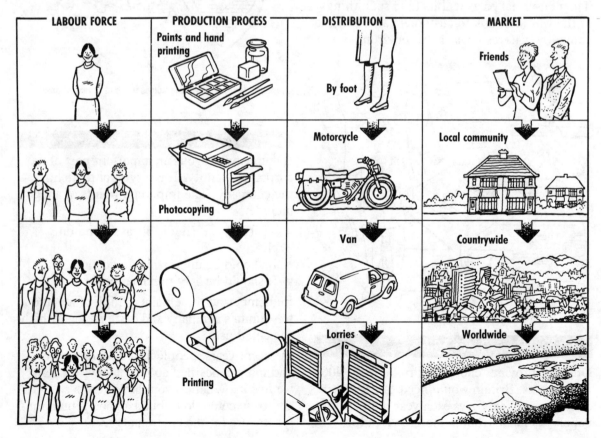

LABOUR FORCE	PRODUCTION PROCESS	DISTRIBUTION	MARKET
	Paints and hand printing	By foot	Friends
	Photocopying	Motorcycle	Local community
		Van	Countrywide
	Printing	Lorries	Worldwide

The Development of a Business: Part 4

1992 and the European Community

The European Community is made up of 12 nations—Belgium, Denmark, France, Germany, Greece, Ireland, Italy, Luxembourg, The Netherlands, Portugal, Spain and the United Kingdom.

Representatives from each of these countries meet at least twice a year to discuss things concerning the Community. New policies and laws are made to help the Community as a whole rather than individual countries.

In 1985 a decision was made to create a single European market by 31 December 1992. The idea was to remove trade barriers between the 12 nations, to increase competition and choice and to offer wider employment opportunities. A treaty was signed with the aim of creating a Europe within which there would be free movement of people, goods and services. The hope was that Europe would become a very powerful economic unit.

2 Shollars each / 4 Lirals each

How might this affect a company?

For UK companies this will mean training staff to speak more languages. They cannot trade with other countries if they can't communicate with them!

There will be a lot more competition within the single market. If other companies abroad offer a better product or service, then they will get the business.

Task

When travelling abroad it can often take some time to get used to a different money system or currency. An item may cost the same in two countries but it will be paid for in two different currencies. We try to work out how much it would cost in our own country by converting the price into our own currency. We can then compare the price with what we would normally pay at home.

The amount of one currency which you can buy with another is called the exchange rate. Bear in mind that this rate can change from time to time.

Design a currency converter which would allow a person to convert easily from one currency into another. You may choose whichever currencies you wish.

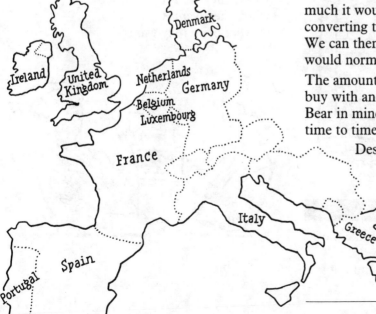

2 Marketing—an Introduction

Markets and Marketing

What is marketing?

As you already know, a **market** is a place where a product or service can be bought (usually for money by a consumer) and sold (usually by a business). The market-place could be a shopping centre, market stall, the high street or anywhere that a product or service is needed.

Strictly speaking, there is a difference between a **customer** and a **consumer**. A customer does not necessarily consume a product. For example, you might buy a birthday present for someone. You are the customer and the other person is the consumer. To avoid confusion, this book will use the word consumer, assuming that the buyer consumes the goods bought.

However, **marketing** is not as simple as this. A business has to get in contact with the person who needs or wants its product.

Marketing would be easy if all the business had to do was to deliver its product and collect the money. Marketing is about bringing the business and consumer together to find out:

what consumers want
where they want it
when they want it
at what price they want it

Fact File

Did you know that Eskimos do not like the idea of selling? They believe that people should give things to other people and not expect anything in return.

Markets and Marketing

Demand

A market is constantly changing. What is fashionable or wanted one day may not be so the next. The consumer and seller have to respond to these changes. For a seller to sell a product or service, there has to be a demand for it. There is no point in developing a product or service if no one will buy it! Sunita found out that there was a need for a particular kind of birthday card. In other words, there was a market for it.

However, demand is not just about wanting a product or service. If this was the case, you could have anything you ever wanted! Demand is also about being able to afford a product or service. No matter how much you want something, if the price is too high you may have to go without or buy a cheaper alternative. Just because a product is cheap, this does not mean it will sell more than a similar, more expensive product. It will only sell if people need it. Therefore, demand is about wanting a product or service *and* having the ability to pay for it at the asking price.

The illustration below shows some of the ways humankind has communicated since the 18th century. It demonstrates that there has always been a need to communicate. The way humankind has communicated has and is still changing.

When you design and develop some of your ideas, remember that people's needs often remain the same; it is the ways of satisfying these needs that change.

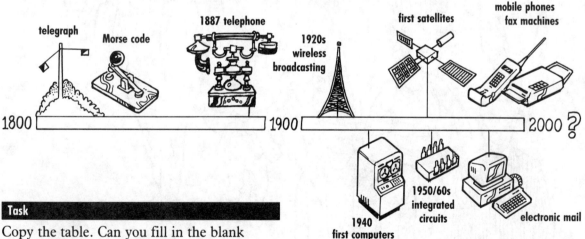

Task

Copy the table. Can you fill in the blank spaces from the list of words available?

filament bulb, typewriter, dustpan and brush, abacus, compact disc, biro

ORIGINAL PRODUCT	REPLACED BY	THE NEED
horse and cart	motor car	travel
candle		light
LP		entertainment
	word processor	information/design
quill pen		writing tool
	calculator	calculations
	Hoover	cleaning

Fact File

The telephone was invented by a British man called Alexander Graham Bell in 1887. He developed the telephone while he worked in North America and Canada. His principle of using a transmitter and receiver is still used in modern-day telephones.

Marketing—an Introduction

Market Research

Market research is about collecting information in order to help a business understand its market. It is an ongoing process and the aim of any market research is to reduce the risks a business has to take when it is developing a product and making it available to a market.

Task

Look at the list of words and the different people. Can you match them together?

a farmer   a salesperson   an athlete   a family a managing director   a builder   an elderly person an engineer   an electrician

Fact File

One of the first uses of market research was to obtain information about the size of the population of countries. This is called a population census.

Only since the 1960s has detailed market research been widely used to help a business find out more about consumers.

Market Research

Consumer research

The illustration and the task of matching show that not all people are the same. People are also consumers. That means consumers are also different. The builder will want a van to carry his tools and materials, the farmer will need a tractor and the athlete might like a sports car!

Obviously, there is not a different market for every consumer. If this were the case, millions of different motor vehicles would have to be made. Groups of people will have different needs. The electrician may need a vehicle he can use for his business which will also be suitable for his private and family use.

It is important to know the different groups of people who make up a market and try to identify their needs. Once the consumers' needs have been identified, the process of developing and making the product can begin.

A market research can be useful to find out the age, sex, size or geographical location (what part of the country people live in) of a market. This information can be useful when you are advertising a product. When you advertise your product, you will want to know where you can reach most of your market.

Task

What papers or magazines do the people in your class/year read? Collect the information, then draw a bar chart showing the results.

Referring to your chart, what advice would you give to a company who wants to place an advertisement in a paper/magazine that will reach an audience of both males and females of your age? Why?

Market Research

Product research

In this kind of research, you will be trying to find out what the market thinks of a product. The product could be a new idea or a development of an existing product. Who will buy the product? Why will they buy it? How much will they be willing to pay? Where is the product to be sold? Could a sample of the market take part in a product analysis?

Market research and questionnaires

The most common way of finding information about a market is by using a questionnaire. A questionnaire is a list of questions which have been carefully thought out. Questions should attempt to gain information about the customer, product or service, or find out anything else which might help to market the product. Market research is of no use if the information it finds out is not understood or needed.

Fact File

Kenneth Grange is a well-known product designer. In 1966 he designed an electric iron, to be sold in Britain and Europe. Market research showed that the British market thought the new open-handle design would not be strong enough. Therefore, a second iron—the same iron but with a closed handle—was designed for the British market.

European market   British market

Therefore, when designing a questionnaire you should consider the following points.

1. What type of questions will be used?

   Structured questions. This type of question requires the respondent (the person who answers the questions) to choose one of the answers provided, usually by ticking a box. It has advantages over other kinds of questionnaire because it is easy to fill in and the answers can be easily analysed. However, the respondents have to choose an answer you have provided, even though they may have different views and the given answers may not represent them.

   How do you commute to school each day?
   - bus
   - car
   - bicycle
   - walk
   - tube/train

   Semi-structured questions. This type of question is similar to structured questions, although there is a space provided if the respondent wants to give a personal reply.

   How much would you pay for the product?
   - between £5-10
   - £10-20
   - £21-30
   - Other price (please specify)

   Open-ended questions. This type of question allows the respondent to express his or her own views in the space provided. However, it takes longer to fill in and the results can be difficult as well as time-consuming to analyse.

   What do you particularly like about the product?
   ....
   ....

Market Research

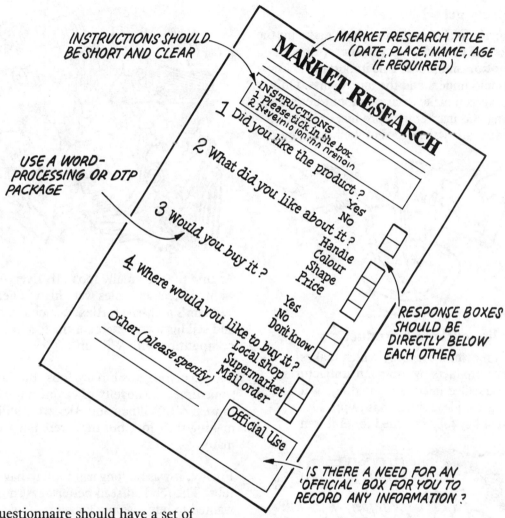

INSTRUCTIONS SHOULD BE SHORT AND CLEAR

MARKET RESEARCH TITLE (DATE, PLACE, NAME, AGE IF REQUIRED)

USE A WORD-PROCESSING OR DTP PACKAGE

RESPONSE BOXES SHOULD BE DIRECTLY BELOW EACH OTHER

IS THERE A NEED FOR AN 'OFFICIAL' BOX FOR YOU TO RECORD ANY INFORMATION?

MARKET RESEARCH

INSTRUCTIONS
1. Please tick in the box
2. Never...

1 Did you like the product?
Yes
No

2 What did you like about it?
Handle
Colour
Shape
Price

3 Would you buy it?
Yes
No
Don't know

4 Where would you like to buy it?
Local shop
Supermarket
Mail order
Other (please specify)

Official Use

2. A questionnaire should have a set of instructions which are clear and easy to follow.

3. Questions should be well spaced. If boxes are used, they should be placed directly below each other. This will make reading the answers afterwards a lot easier. Try to use a word-processing or desktop publishing package.

4. A questionnaire should not take a long time to fill in, otherwise the respondent may lose interest.

Task

Now you know a lot more about market research and questionnaires, what would you change in the questionnaire you designed for Sunita?

The Marketing Mix

The product

There are four ingredients which make up the **marketing mix**: they are **product**, **price**, **promotion** and **place**. It is important to know about and understand the ingredients. Only then can you make decisions about designing, making and marketing a product or service that will satisfy the needs of your consumers.

The life-cycle of a product

William owns a company which makes various products by using a manufacturing method called injection moulding. William had a great idea, which was to produce unusual key fobs intended for children.

At first the fobs really took off. Everyone wanted them and sales were high. Then William's arch-rival, Alex, decided to make and sell his own version of the fob in **competition** with William.

Soon everyone was buying fobs. But, after some time, the novelty of having a fob began to wear off. William and Alex were still making their fobs but they were not selling as many.

Finally, it was no longer trendy to have these fobs. The fob had seen better days; no one wanted to buy one any longer.

The Marketing Mix

The story of the fobs is an example of a **product life-cycle**. There are five stages in this life-cycle.

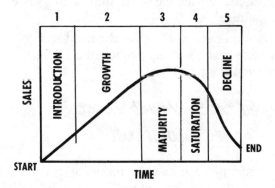

Stage 1

This is when the product is introduced. Not many people will know about it so lots of money will have to be spent on advertising to promote the product and increase people's awareness of it.

Stage 2

This is the growth stage. Sales are increasing. Competitors introduce their own versions. However, this may be an ideal time to introduce another style or a variation of the product.

Stage 3

The product reaches maturity. Sales are at their highest.

Stage 4

This is saturation point. Sales begin to decline due to such things as too many competitors trying to sell the product and not enough customers or the craze coming to an end.

Stage 5

With declining sales, the product will no longer make a profit and will be taken off the market. The length of time a life-cycle lasts varies between products. One thing that is certain is that all products have a life-cycle.

If only William had known about product life cycles. He could have made the life-cycle last longer by introducing another or an improved fob at the right time. If he had done some market research, it might have told him that there was a market for a dual-purpose fob and eraser.

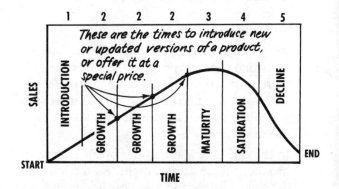

These are the times to introduce new or updated versions of a product, or offer it at a special price.

Task

Can you answer one of William's possible research questions?

What time of year would you introduce the eraser fob?

1. End of the school term?
2. Beginning of the school term?
3. Don't know?
4. During the holidays?

Explain your answer in two or three sentences.

25

The Marketing Mix

Price

The pricing of a product is an important ingredient in the marketing mix. Price must not be confused with cost. In order to calculate the price of a product, that is, what it will be sold for, the total cost of things like materials and wages has to be found. Costs can be divided into two categories, **fixed costs** and **variable costs**.

Fixed costs

These are costs that will not change as output increases. For example, rent and employees' salaries always have to be paid.

Variable costs

As you might have guessed, variable costs are costs that change as output increases. As more products are made, more raw materials, for example, will be needed. In other words, variable costs will increase as production increases.

In the early stage of Sunita's business, she produced three cards a night. As the business developed, more and more cards were being made. Therefore, more and more materials such as card, paints, brushes and pencils were needed. Her variable costs continuously increased.

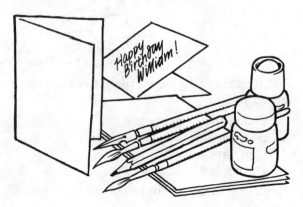

Working out total costs

In this section, the word 'unit' is used instead of the words 'pence' or 'pounds'. If you are confused, replace the word 'unit' with 'pence' or 'pounds'.

Once you have worked out the fixed and variable costs, add the two together. This will give you the total cost.

$$fixed\ cost + variable\ cost = total\ cost$$

For example, Sunita was producing cards using a photocopier and her costs were:

fixed costs (e.g. her friend's wages)
  200 units
and variable costs (e.g. materials)
  100 units
Total cost: 200 + 100 = 300

What would the total cost of one card be if Sunita produced 30 cards? To find the cost of one card, we simply divide the total cost by the number of products made:

$$300 \div 30 = 10$$

The cost to produce 1 card is 10 units

The Marketing Mix

Price and profit

To fix a price for each card, Sunita has to decide how much to add on to the cost of each card. This is known as the **profit element**. There are different ways of deciding how to work out the profit element.

A new product

If a product is new, lots of people will want it. Therefore, Sunita could decide to make the profit element 4 units rather than 2 or 3. People might be willing to pay this because they would not be able to buy the same product from anyone else.

$$10 + 4 = 14$$

The price for each card will be 14 units.

Adding a percentage

Sunita could have worked this out by using percentages. If the profit element was set at 40 per cent on each card then:

The total cost of each card is 10 units.

The profit element has been fixed at 40 per cent.

$$\frac{\overset{1}{\cancel{10}} \times 40}{\underset{10}{\cancel{100}}} = \frac{40}{10} = 4$$

The profit element is 4. Therefore the price of each card will be 14 units.

The consumer

What the consumer thinks is also important. For example, if you fix the price too high, many customers may buy an alternative. If you fix the price too low, the customer may become suspicious and think that perhaps the quality will be low.

Task

At first William made 600 fobs each day. His costs were as follows:

fixed costs : 1100 units
variable costs : 1300 units

Work out:

1. The total cost, if he was producing 600 fobs a day.
2. The cost of each fob.
3. The price of each fob, if he fixed the profit element at 50 per cent.

27

The Marketing Mix

Promotion

Promotion deals with how a business communicates with customers.

Advertising

Advertising usually describes the product in some way or explains to the consumer the benefits of a product. Most advertisements use a persuasive message to promote their product or service.

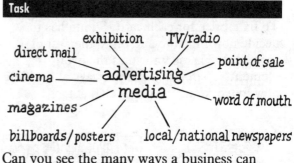

direct mail — exhibition — TV/radio — point of sale — cinema — **advertising media** — word of mouth — magazines — billboards/posters — local/national newspapers

Can you see the many ways a business can promote its product or service? The spider diagram may help you. Choose one method of advertising and try to find out more about it.

The Romans advertised—they informed people about forthcoming gladiator contests by painting messages on walls.

The Marketing Mix

Things to remember

1. Identify your audience. Remember the different groups of people. These people can be reached in different ways. It is important to know where they can be reached. What papers do they read? What radio/TV stations do they listen to and at what times?
2. It is important to realize that the message you use to advertise a product will be different depending on the audience. For example, advertising to teenagers will differ from advertising to their parents.

Sales promotion

A sales promotion attempts to persuade the consumer to buy now rather than later. There are many ways this can be done.

The worst time of the year for computer sales is usually the summer months. If a computer manufacturer launches a sales promotion then, it can be a way of maintaining the public's interest in his product. It can also be a strategy for keeping (or getting) customers from his competitors.

Some good things about advertising:

1. Advertising tells people about products, services or information they may need to know.
2. Advertising makes life more colourful.
3. Advertising may increase the amount of products sold. This could mean the price of the product is reduced.

Some bad things about advertising:

1. The cost of advertising will increase the cost of the product. This means the consumer will have to pay more.
2. Some advertisements may not tell the whole truth.
3. Only the bigger businesses can afford to pay the high costs of advertising.

What can you add to these two lists?

Task

Get into groups of between three and four people. Choose one good and one bad thing about advertising from the list above or from other aspects of it you have considered. Discuss them, making sure one member of the group is writing down the main points. The chairperson in each group should then share the group's findings with the class and answer any questions.

The Marketing Mix

Place

Thè final ingredient in the marketing mix is place. It involves the **distribution** of products. Distribution is all about getting products to where they are needed. This can take one step, but usually involves more.

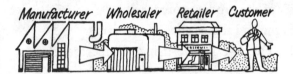

Manufacturer   Wholesaler   Retailer   Customer

The manufacturer makes the products. The manufacturer has no room at the factory to store the products and sells them to a **wholesaler**, who stores the products in a **warehouse**. The wholesaler will then sell the products to the **retailer**, for example, shop owners near by. The retailer sells the products to the consumers (you and me).

The distribution between each stage should be planned carefully. What modes (types) of transport will be needed? How much will it cost? How will this affect the total cost? What are the delivery times between each stage? If a delivery from the wholesaler is delivered at the wrong time the shopkeeper may lose customers. A shop selling, for example, sunglasses would want to have them in stock in the summer, not the winter.

Distribution also involves customer service. This means considering the needs of the customer. A pizza restaurant may provide a take-away service, so the customers may like to know:

1. Can you deliver pizzas? If so, will this service be free?
2. How quick will the service be?

Different customers will have different priorities. It is up to the restaurant owner to find out what they are.

The Business Plan

Before any business is set up it is important to put together a **business plan**. A business plan should show:

1. What you know about the market, the marketing mix and your product or service.
2. A **forecast** of what your cash flow will be over a period of time. In other words, how much money will you need to start your business and how much money do you expect to get in return? These are known as cash outflow and cash inflow.

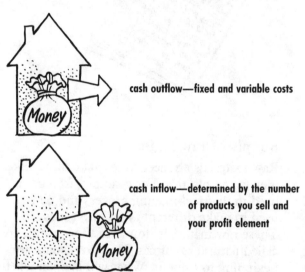

cash outflow—fixed and variable costs

cash inflow—determined by the number of products you sell and your profit element

We already know that Sunita's outflow (total cost) was 300 units when she produced 30 cards. If she fixed her profit element at 4 units and she sold all 30 cards, her total incomings would be 420 units.

Sunita's forecasts showed that her incomings were higher than her outgoings. There is not much point in setting up a business if your incomings are less than your outgoings!

When Sunita was producing 30 cards a night, her cash outflow and inflow were:

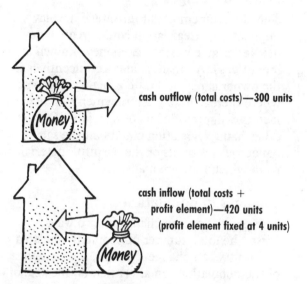

cash outflow (total costs)—300 units

cash inflow (total costs + profit element)—420 units (profit element fixed at 4 units)

Therefore, Sunita's profit was 120 units on every 30 cards she sold.

Task

Now you know a lot more about marketing, what advice would you give to William if he had another chance?

Market research is not a one-off activity. It can provide a business with up-to-date information about a market which is constantly changing. Forecasts should be evaluated on a regular basis and changes made if necessary.

Marketing—an Introduction

The Business Environment

So far we have looked at how a business can make some decisions about the ingredients of the marketing mix. However, there are some factors over which a business has little or no control.

Political changes

The Government could introduce new laws (**legislation**). Legislation could create a new market or give businesses money (known as **incentives**). A business may get incentives if the owner agrees to locate a factory in a place where there is high unemployment—a new factory will provide lots of new jobs. On the other hand, legislation could ban the sale of dangerous products or the harmful materials from which they are made.

Changes in population

The population can change in two ways. First, the total number of people in one area or country can change. Second, the structure of the population can alter, that is, the size of the groups within it can change. How many males/females or young/old are there? Population changes are very important as they affect the supply of labour. Labour refers to the people who are of working age. It is known that in the 1990s there will be a fall in the number of people aged between 16 and 19.

Supply of raw materials

Raw materials are needed to make things like metals and plastics. For example, iron ore is used in the steel-making process and oil is used to make different types of plastics.
These raw materials, found in the ground, are called natural resources. However, some are beginning to run out. What will happen when they are all used up?

Task

What types of industries employ people between the ages of 16 and 19?

How will these industries be affected by the fall in numbers during the 1990s?

32

The Business Environment

Technological changes

The greatest development in technology in recent times is the microchip. Microchips are electronic circuits that are so small you cannot see them with the naked human eye. They are also called integrated circuits (ICs). Integrated circuits are used in everyday items such as calculators and personal stereos. Their use has also changed the way industry works and makes things.

To illustrate this point, let us look at the different printing methods Sunita used.

1. The diagram illustrates the production methods used by Sunita. She carefully planned each stage, forecasting her cash outflow and cash inflow. As the business developed she became aware of the technology available to her. At first, Sunita reproduced her cards by drawing each one. This is the oldest method of reproducing drawings and was used until the advent of wooden printing blocks many hundreds of years ago. As her business developed, Sunita used modern black and white and colour photocopiers.

Finally, Sunita got a printing business to do the printing for her. Modern printing techniques are computerized. An example of this is newspaper production.

2. Developments in technology can also result in the death of old products and the birth of new ones. For example, look what the microchip did to our poor old friend William!

DRAWING BY HAND
(Stencils)
⇩
PHOTOCOPYING
(Black and white)
⇩
PHOTOCOPYING
(Colour)
⇩
PRINTING MACHINE
(Second-hand)
⇩
PRINTING BUSINESS
(Outside)

Task

Find out a little more about newspaper production methods. List some of the advantages that modern, computerized newspaper production methods have over the traditional methods. Can you list any disadvantages?

3 Design for Manufacture

The Pizza Parlour

When a new product is being designed, the designers have to think about many things apart from the product itself. For example, they have to decide which processes will be used to make the product. A manufacturing process suitable for making a fairly small number of items may not be suitable for a large number. The choice of process will depend upon the number of products being made, that is, on the **production run**.

The designers will also need to think about what the consumer requires of the product. This may include such things as the appearance of the product (colour scheme, surface texture, form, etc.), how long the product will last, the effect of the product and its production process on the environment, and so on.

The packaging of the product will also have to be designed, sometimes by a different group of designers. The packaging will be subject to similar considerations to the product itself. This chapter looks at some of the different things which must be taken into account when a product is designed to be manufactured. In this example the product is a pizza which will be sold from a small town-centre take-away called 'The Pizza Parlour'.

Fact File

- Had we lived in Roman times, we would have tucked into camels' heels, larks' tongues and humming birds in walnut shells rather than our take-away pizzas.

The Pizza Parlour Recipe

This is the recipe which the parlour has decided to use for its pizzas:

Base

0.25 pint water
0.5 teaspoon sugar
1.5 teaspoons dried yeast
0.5 lb plain flour
1 teaspoon salt
Knob of lard
Cooking oil

Method for base

Warm the water to blood heat and dissolve the sugar in it. Sprinkle on the dried yeast and leave the mixture in a warm place until it becomes frothy. Mix the flour and salt together and rub in the lard. Mix in the yeast mixture and beat until the dough doesn't stick to the sides of the bowl. Knead the dough on a floured board until it becomes smooth and elastic. Put the dough in an oiled plastic bag and leave it in a warm place until it has doubled in size. Turn the dough onto a floured surface and roll it into a long strip. Brush it with oil and roll it up like a Swiss roll. Grease a 30-cm plain flan ring, put it onto a greased baking sheet and roll out the dough to fit the ring. Brush the surface of the dough with oil.

Basic topping

1 onion
2 cloves of garlic
Chopped tomatoes
0.5 lb mozzarella cheese
Tomato purée
Salt and pepper
Basil, oregano, bay leaves
Sunflower oil

Method for topping

Chop up the onion and garlic and fry them in oil. Add the chopped tomatoes and a squirt of tomato purée, along with a little salt and pepper, a teaspoon of chopped basil and 2 or 3 bay leaves. Leave the mixture to heat for about 20 minutes and then add a tablespoon of chopped oregano. Remove the bay leaves after about 2 minutes and pour the topping over the base. Cook the pizza in the oven for about 15 minutes (gas mark 8, 230 °C/450 °F) before adding the grated mozzarella cheese. Return the pizza to the oven for a further 10 minutes.

Design for Manufacture

The Pizza Parlour Recipe

Study the two methods carefully for a minute or two. Which parts of these processes do you think will be most difficult? Assuming that many such pizzas will need to be made in a short period of time, what problems are likely to occur?

The pizza bases, for example, take a long time to make and people might not be prepared to wait. Many ingredients are required and so care would be needed to ensure that none of these ran out. They could be ordered in large quantities (bulk ordering) but extra storage space would then be needed. Over-ordering might result in some ingredients going stale before they were used.

An estimate would need to be made as to how many pizzas would be sold each day. How do you think The Pizza Parlour could estimate how many pizzas it might sell in one week?

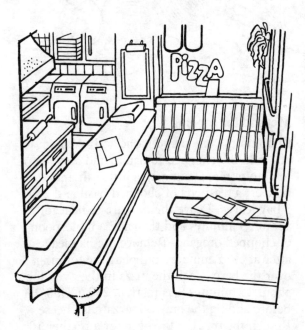

Task

The inside of The Pizza Parlour needs to be designed carefully. The ingredients should be within easy reach of the cook and there should be plenty of work space. A cash till will be needed and perhaps even seating for people who are waiting for their take-away food.

Taking these points into consideration, design an interior for The Pizza Parlour. Use drawings and models to illustrate your designs.

Types of Production

The Pizza Parlour would need to be well organized so that customers were not kept waiting too long. Any company which is not well organized will find it difficult to sell goods and may go out of business. There are three main ways of producing goods in today's world of production. Which of these do you think would apply at The Pizza Parlour?

Mass production

Mass production is a method whereby many identical products are made as cheaply as possible. Mass production usually makes use of long production lines to produce such things as cars, hi-fi systems, chocolate bars or records. Liquids and semi-liquids may also be made in this way, such as paint, shampoo or medicines. The process is then called continuous flow production.

Mass production normally uses more machine labour than human labour and some processes are completely automated. Many production lines are kept running continuously because it is costly to stop them. Careful planning is therefore necessary.

Job production

Job production is the term used when individual items are made to a special set of requirements. Job production would include such things as made-to-measure suits and furniture, the building of a bridge or the painting of a picture. Each item made is different and will usually involve a lot of human labour.

Batch production

Batch production applies to products which are made in large but limited numbers. Aeroplanes, furniture or certain fashion clothes, for example, may be produced using such a production process. The demand may not be great enough to have the product mass produced but it might, instead, be made in batches.

Design for Manufacture

Consumer Requirements

There are many different things which affect how well a product sells. One of the most important things is whether it meets the needs of the buyer. This means more than simply whether the product works well or not. These factors are called the consumer requirements. What kind of consumer requirements do you think The Pizza Parlour should consider?

The product itself

If the pizzas are to sell then they will obviously need to be made well. But what is a 'good' pizza? Ask some of your friends what they think is the mark of a good pizza. Perhaps some will like thin, crispy pizzas with a plain topping. Others may like a thicker 'deep pan' pizza with several toppings.

A range of pizzas may, therefore, need to be offered in different sizes to give the consumer some choice. Vegetarians will need to be catered for, which means that meat-free pizzas should be available. The pizzas should be served nice and hot, and it might be a good idea to slice the pizza into manageable segments which are easier to eat.

It might also be necessary to cater for the health-conscious by including a small salad bar. Salad often makes a nice addition to a meal as well as being a meal in itself and will help to promote a shop's healthy image.

Consumer Requirements

Packaging

The pizza packaging creates one or two environmental considerations. We are becoming more and more aware of our environment and do not like to see it harmed. We do not like to see resources wasted or used unnecessarily. Therefore, the packaging should not be excessive and could, perhaps, be made of a **biodegradable** material.

Recycled card might be a suitable material for part of the packaging. However, it would be necessary to check current laws about the sale of food in recycled containers. Whichever material is used for the packaging, it should ensure that the pizza stays hot and should not allow any grease to get through to the outside.

The packaging should be easy to dispose of, and if rubbish bins are placed outside The Pizza Parlour customers could be encouraged not to litter the streets. To keep local residents happy, a litter patrol could be set up to keep the streets free of misplaced used packaging.

The ingredients and nutritional information about the pizza might be included as part of the packaging. Many people these days like to know the contents of what they are eating.

Other customer requirements

There are other things to think about for the service of the pizza. People do not like waiting and so a fast service would be needed with the facility to place orders by telephone. A home-delivery service could be offered, whereby pizzas are delivered by motor bike.

The sale of drinks may also be considered because many people like a drink with their food. Drinks can be very profitable for a business because little preparation is required. Other **consumer requirements** will be a clean, fresh preparation and service area and, of course, the food must be competitively priced.

Fact File

- Every year we get through about six million tonnes of packaging in the UK.
- Packaging makes up about a third of the rubbish by weight which we throw in our dustbins.

Design for Manufacture

Packaging the Pizza

The Pizza Parlour will need to decide how it is going to package the take-away food. As well as the consumer requirements suggested previously, there will be the practical considerations. The packaging must protect the pizza and keep it fresh and hygienic. It should be cheap to produce so that little is added to the cost of the pizza.

It must also be easy to store, taking up as little room as possible. Since the pizzas are made in different sizes, a range of packaging will need to be produced.

Material	Advantage	Disadvantage
Biscuit tin		
Wooden box		
Plastic bag		
Gold bar		
Cork		
Glass dish		

Task

Study the sample materials illustrated here. Which of these would be suitable for packaging the take-away pizzas? List the advantages and disadvantages of each.

Which materials would you use for the packaging? If the packaging was actually made at The Pizza Parlour then a lot of money might be saved by not having to pay another company. How might the packaging be designed so that it could be made 'in-house'?

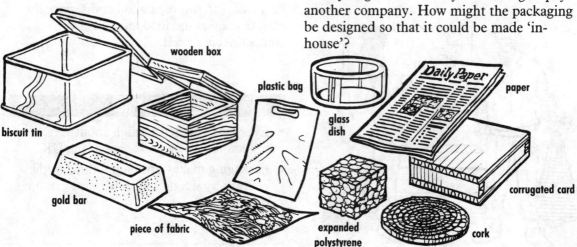

wooden box

plastic bag

glass dish

paper

biscuit tin

gold bar

piece of fabric

expanded polystyrene

cork

corrugated card

Packaging the Pizza

Time could be used during quiet periods to prepare the packaging for later use. What times of the day would you expect to be the quiet periods? A lot of take-away places like to stay open until after 11 p.m. This is because they make a great deal of money from people leaving pubs and entertainment centres as they are closing. However, many such places are not allowed to open at this time, particularly in residential areas. Why do you think this is?

Whichever design is used for the packaging, it must be quick and easy to make up. For example, if the packaging is designed as a

Obviously, it will take a while to make each individual package whichever method is used. This is time which could be used for other duties and time which must be paid for by The Pizza Parlour. A comparison will need to be made between the costs of paying an outsider to make the packaging and making it in-house.

card development then the process could be speeded up by using a template. Each development would be marked out individually and cut out using a scalpel or scissors. The developments could be stored flat to save space and folded as needed.

In the example below, 18 pizzas would need to be sold to cover the cost of making the packaging for a hundred pizzas. So long as this amounts to less than buying the pre-made packaging and does not use time needed for other duties then a saving will be made.

100 pieces of card

4 pizzas

marking and cutting materials

3 pizzas

labour

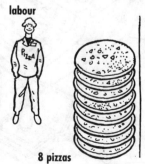

8 pizzas

printing kit

3 pizzas

Design for Manufacture

Information Design

Careful thought will need to be given to deciding what information the customers of The Pizza Parlour will want to have. Obvious examples are the range of food and drink on offer and the prices of these items. This information may be shown on a large display board as well as being printed on small menus for customers to take away.

Other types of information may be a description of the ingredients of the food, nutrition information and special meal deals. How might this information be presented? What production methods could be used? Listed below are some alternatives.

Think about groups of people with special needs when designing information systems.

Pen and paper
Chalk and chalkboard
Dry-wipe marker and board

Typewriter
Computer and printer
Rubber-stamp printing set

Which information system do you think would be most suitable for The Pizza Parlour? Many companies are now investing in their own desktop publishing systems, which can be an effective and professional way of providing information. The initial costs for equipment are high but new designs can be created as necessary without the expenses of traditional printing.

Desktop Publishing

Desktop publishing is a system in which pages of text and/or graphics are designed and arranged on a page layout using a computer and are then printed on a printer connected to it. All of the work, from the initial design stage to the final printout, can take place at a desk. This would be a typical approach to desktop publishing:

Text is typed into the computer using a word-processing software package. The text is spell-checked but no attention is paid to the size or style of the text on the screen at this stage. The aim is simply to get all of the information into the machine.

Graphic images may be created by using a drawing software package on the computer. Alternatively, existing images (such as photographs) can be fed into the computer through a process called scanning. Scanned images are saved by the computer as a collection of thousands of tiny dots, usually black and white. The more dots making up the image the better the image will appear. However, scanned images can use up a lot of the computer's memory.

The text and graphics are combined, using a page-making software package. The text can be chopped up and moved about on the screen and the size and style of type can be changed. The graphic images may also be re-sized and moved about on the screen. The moving and re-sizing operation continues until a suitable layout is achieved.

The page is printed out. The quality of the print will depend on the quality of the printer. Laser printers can have a very high resolution and produce excellent results. Multiple copies can be produced if necessary, or a single copy may be produced and photocopied as many times as needed.

Design for Manufacture

Nutrition Information

In today's health-conscious world people have become much more choosy about what they eat. If we eat a well-balanced diet and take regular exercise we have a better chance of living a fit and healthy life. The Pizza Parlour decided to find out more about what its food contained and what its **nutritional value** was.

Fibre

Fibre is found in foods which grow from the ground, such as cereals, beans, peas, vegetables and fruit. Fibre-rich foods are very important for good health and can be filling without being fattening. Such foods will also contain lots of vitamins and other nutrients.

Sugar

Sugar gives us energy but provides no other nutrients such as vitamins, minerals, fibre or protein. Too much sugar promotes tooth decay and can lead to problems of overweight.

Fat

There are basically two types of fat, called saturated and unsaturated fats. The difference is in their chemical make-up. Saturated fats are found in meat and in dairy products like milk, cheese and butter. They are also found in cakes and chocolates. Unsaturated fats contain essential fatty acids, which are important for good health and cannot be made in the body. They are found in fish such as herring, mackerel and trout as well as in nuts and certain margarines.

Eating too much fat leads to overweight. The more saturated fat we eat, the more cholesterol builds up in the bloodstream. This can eventually block up the arteries and may be a cause of heart disease. Unsaturated fats do not have the same effect and help to repair our body cells.

Salt

We all need some salt but we normally get enough from our food without having to add any extra. Too much salt can lead to high blood pressure, which can cause heart disease and strokes.

A range of foods which are rich in sugar.

chocolate

biscuits   tins of drink   cakes

Nutrition Information

Additives

Additives may be added to foods for a number of reasons. They can preserve food, add to the flavour or alter the colour. They are normally listed with the ingredients and are shown by their European Community number (the E number). Such additives have been tested and passed for use in the EC.

This tells you how many joules there are in 100 g of the product. Joules are used to measure energy.

This shows how much energy is provided by 100 g of the product. Here the energy is measured in calories.

Carbohydrates contain sugar and starch. Here we can see how much of the carbohydrate is sugar.

This tells you how much saturated fat there is in 100 g of the product.

NUTRITION INFORMATION
100 g (just under 4 oz) give you:

Energy	1440 kJ / 340 kcal	
Protein	12.3 g	
Carbohydrate	65.4 g	
of which sugars	5.2 g	
	4.9 g	
Fat	0.7 g	
of which saturates	0.3 g	
Sodium	13.2 g	
Fibre		

This shows the amount of salt.

We should try to eat 30 g of fibre each day.

Task

Using a desktop publishing system, The Pizza Parlour could quickly make up a leaflet to provide information about the range of food, prices and nutrition content.

Design such a leaflet for The Pizza Parlour, remembering that it could be folded in a number of ways. If you have access to a computer with page-making software, then use that. If not, the text can be typed or hand-written and pasted onto the page. Make up your own names for the different pizzas but try to base the nutrition information on a typical medium-size pizza.

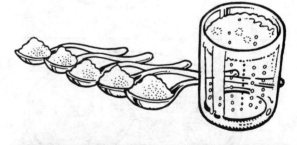

Fact File

A glass of an ordinary soft drink contains about 5 teaspoonfuls of sugar. The bacteria in our mouths feed on this sugar and produce acids which eat into our teeth!

45

Design for Manufacture

Running The Pizza Parlour

Large-scale production

The average cost of producing a single pizza at The Pizza Parlour can easily be worked out. This is done by dividing all the costs of The Pizza Parlour over the period of, say, one month by the number of pizzas produced during this time. The **average cost** for each pizza will change as the number of pizzas sold changes. This is because, as output increases, the fixed costs such as rent and wages are divided between a larger number of pizzas.

For example, in March, The Pizza Parlour might have sold 500 pizzas. The fixed costs will therefore be divided by 500. In May, it might have sold 1000 pizzas. In this case, the fixed costs will be divided by 1000, which will result in a smaller amount. The average cost for each pizza will, therefore, be reduced. This is called the economies of scale. As the scale of production increases, the average cost falls.

Competition

Any value which is added to the pizzas above the average cost will be the profit element. The price of the pizza is set by adding the cost and profit element together. If the average cost is reduced but the price remains unchanged then the profit element will be greater.

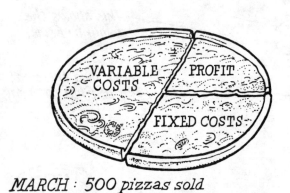

MARCH : 500 pizzas sold

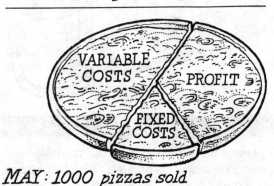

MAY : 1000 pizzas sold

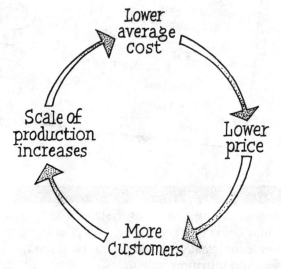

Most businesses will aim for the lowest average cost so that a low price can be set without losing profit. If a lower price is set, more people will be tempted to buy The Pizza Parlour's pizzas, which means that the scale of production will increase and the average cost will be further reduced. Setting lower prices than others do is a major element of competition between companies.

Running The Pizza Parlour

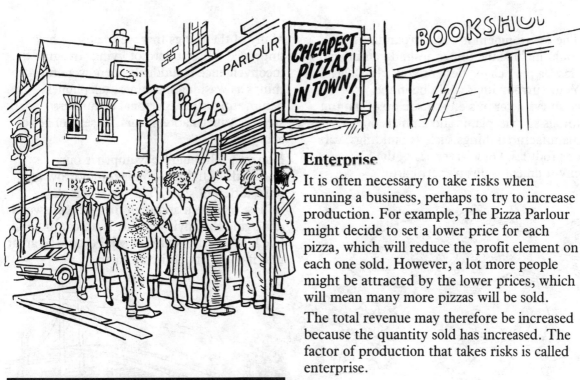

Enterprise

It is often necessary to take risks when running a business, perhaps to try to increase production. For example, The Pizza Parlour might decide to set a lower price for each pizza, which will reduce the profit element on each one sold. However, a lot more people might be attracted by the lower prices, which will mean many more pizzas will be sold.

The total revenue may therefore be increased because the quantity sold has increased. The factor of production that takes risks is called enterprise.

Task

If you were setting up a take-away pizza place in the same area as The Pizza Parlour, what steps would you take to attract and keep customers? Write a plan outline for your business which explains how you would compete with The Pizza Parlour.

4 Marketing and the Environment

What Is the Environment?

The **environment** is our surroundings. It could include the things around you in your class, a pen, chair, desk or your classmates! Your surroundings could be in the countryside or in a city, made up of natural things such as plants and animals or manufactured things such as buildings, cars or products. On a larger scale, the environment is our planet, Earth.

Many of the things that we use today have improved our standard of living. Imagine the inconvenience if suddenly there were no such things as washing machines, telephones, denim, tracksuits, personal computers/ stereos, supermarkets, cars, buses, lorries or aeroplanes.

However, although they improve our standards of living for today, tomorrow may tell a different story. The way we make things, use them and then throw them away is damaging the environment. If we continue to live like this, the damage will become so great that it could affect life on earth.

Acorn

Oakleaf

Leaf

Cone

What Is the Environment?

How paper is made

Before we look at how our planet is changing, let's look at an example of how one particular product is made. This is a simplified description of how paper is manufactured.

1. Trees (usually evergreen) are cut down and taken to a paper-mill, where the bark is stripped off and the trunk is cut up into smaller, more manageable logs.
2. The logs are fed into a machine which breaks them down into pieces a few centimetres long.
3. The small pieces are put into a mixture of hot water and chemicals and turned into a pulp. The pulp is then washed and bleached several times.
4. The pulp is broken down further into small fibres.
5. The fibres are mixed with more water. Coloured paper is made by adding dyes at this stage.
6. The water is drained away and the fibres are passed through a set of heated rollers. The rollers have two functions. They press the fibres together while at the same time the heat evaporates any water that has not already been drained away.
7. The paper is now ready to be used to make things like books and packaging material.

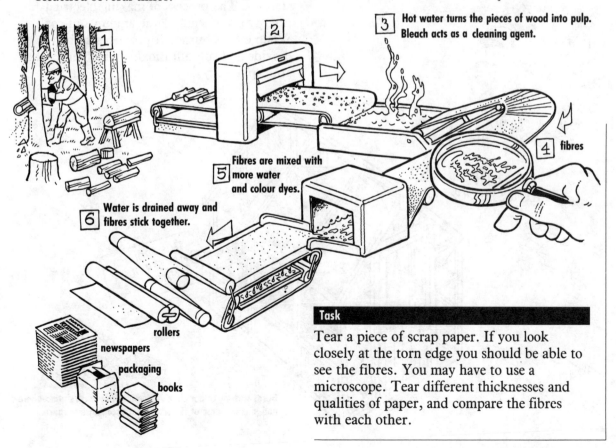

3 Hot water turns the pieces of wood into pulp. Bleach acts as a cleaning agent.

4 fibres

5 Fibres are mixed with more water and colour dyes.

6 Water is drained away and fibres stick together.

rollers

newspapers

packaging

books

Task

Tear a piece of scrap paper. If you look closely at the torn edge you should be able to see the fibres. You may have to use a microscope. Tear different thicknesses and qualities of paper, and compare the fibres with each other.

Marketing and the Environment

Damaging the Environment

The greenhouse effect

The air inside a greenhouse warms up as the heat from the sun shines through the glass. Not much of the heat escapes back through the glass. The warm air inside becomes trapped. This is how a greenhouse works, creating a warm climate so plants are protected from the cold weather.

Now imagine that the earth is surrounded by a giant greenhouse. The earth's **atmosphere** acts like the glass. It allows light and heat from the sun in but only lets a little heat escape. This is how the atmosphere works and its presence is essential. Without it there would be no life on earth.

However, humankind is beginning to notice that the atmosphere is changing. One reason for this change is that certain gases (for example, carbon dioxide) are rising into the atmosphere, acting as a barrier, and allowing even less of the sun's heat to escape back into space. The earth is warming up! This is known as the **greenhouse effect**. It is causing global warming and it is believed that some of the ice around the North and South Poles is melting. This will mean that sea levels will rise and parts of many countries will be under water. The earth's climate may also change.

Humans get their **energy** by eating nutritious food. Many machines get their energy from electricity, which is produced in power stations. The process of making electricity can involve burning large amounts of coal. When coal is burned it produces carbon dioxide and sulphur dioxide which enter the atmosphere.

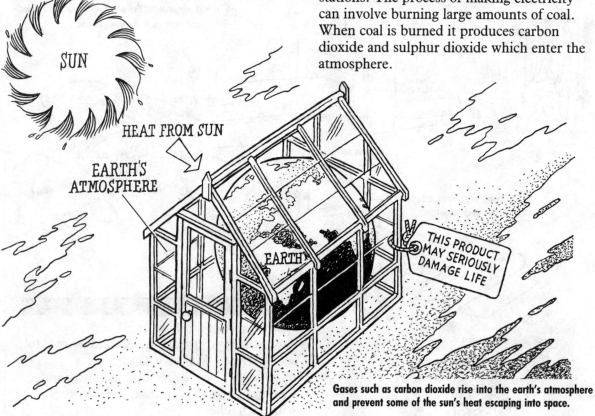

Gases such as carbon dioxide rise into the earth's atmosphere and prevent some of the sun's heat escaping into space.

Damaging the Environment

Acid rain

Coal is one type of **fossil fuel**. Other types of fossil fuel are oil and natural gas. When these are burned they produce a gas called nitrogen oxide. This gas rises into the air and mixes with sulphur dioxide and the water vapour found in clouds. The mixture forms an acid solution which falls back to earth as **acid rain**. Acid rain is responsible for damaging buildings, killing forests, wildlife and polluting lakes and rivers (resulting in fish dying).

Reproduced by kind permission of Greenpeace Ltd.

Fact File

Did you know that even if the poisonous gases were removed from the air tomorrow it would still take thirty years for the lakes and rivers to recover!

The ozone layer

Ozone is a gas similar to oxygen. It surrounds the earth, forming the **ozone layer**, which protects our planet from harmful ultraviolet (UV) sun rays. UV light is not too damaging in *very small* doses. It is the light that gives people suntans. However, too much exposure to UV light can cause problems such as skin cancer in people and dramatic changes in our climate.

Large holes are beginning to appear in the ozone layer. This is because of chemicals called chloro-fluoro-carbons or CFCs, for short. They are found in things like aerosol sprays, egg cartons, refrigerators and hamburger cartons. As a result of public awareness of the damage being caused, most aerosols made today do not contain CFCs.

Fact File

Wastes discharged from factories into rivers can reduce the oxygen level, pollute the water and kill fish and other creatures. However, where clean-up campaigns have reduced or stopped these discharges, fish are beginning to appear again in rivers which previously seemed to be dead.

Consumers and the Environment

Green consumerism

Consumers nowadays are more aware of the harm that humankind is doing to the environment than they were twenty years ago. This is partly due to coverage by the media in TV and radio programmes and newspaper and magazine articles. This increased awareness has resulted in customers buying products that they know are less harmful to the environment. Consumers are now asking questions about a product before they buy it. How is it made? What is it made from? What will happen to the packaging? More and more people are becoming **green consumers**. Marketing is all about identifying customers' needs and wants and bringing a product to them at the right time and in the right place. Any company which fails to do this may not survive.

Companies are becoming more responsible. This increased responsibility improves the image of a business with consumers. A business shows it is aware, caring and doing something for the future of our planet. A good example of such a company is the Body Shop.

Task

Have you noticed how many products inform the consumer that they are friendly towards the environment? Make a list of the different types of messages that claim to be 'environmentally friendly'. Look for the more unusual ones, such as detergents that are 'phosphate free' and batteries that are 'mercury free'. Do you understand all or some of these messages? Is it important to display this information and if so, why?

Fact File

In a recent survey about packaging, 60 per cent of people said they would be willing to buy a product if they knew the packaging would cause less harm to the environment.

Government and the Environment

Government legislation

Legislation simply means the passing of laws. Governments all over the world are acting, sometimes with each other, to reduce the harm to the environment.

Governments also take other types of action. They can encourage businesses to use recycled materials by giving them incentives.

Local councils (and some industries) sponsor schemes, such as collection points for glass (bottlebanks) and waste paper. Some councils also collect waste metal and plastic. Find out if there are similar schemes in your area.

A business may feel that it is necessary to make changes because of the changing attitudes of consumers. Government legislation may also force a business to make changes.

Design and the Environment

Green design

The job of the designer is to design a product that will work efficiently (function), and be safe and reliable to use. However, the designer will also consider things like the needs and wants of the consumer. He or she will be interested in information from market research, and will also be involved in promoting the product or service (displaying and advertising). Designing and marketing are closely linked.

Biodegradable means a material which decomposes or breaks up in the environment. Even certain plastics are biodegradable.

Buying unbleached and undyed fabrics, especially cotton, will reduce pollution.

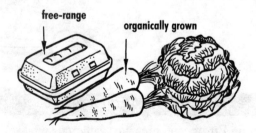

To make foam boxes requires more energy than to make cardboard boxes.

The way food is produced is also important. What do 'free-range' and 'organically grown' mean?

Concentrated products can be used to refill the original container. Just add water! This helps reduce packaging waste.

Until recently, most designers probably did not consider environmental issues to be very important. However, environmental issues are now part of the design process, alongside performance, cost, the materials and processes used and aesthetic appeal. This page shows some examples of **green design**.

The automotive (car) industry has been aware of environmental issues for some time. Cars are more fuel-efficient thanks to:
(i) the use of lighter materials, e.g. plastic body parts. Ford has already developed an all-plastic engine!
(ii) aerodynamics—reduces 'drag'.
Cars also use and produce fewer toxic substances, e.g.
● solvents in body paints
● lead-free petrol
● catalytic converters (reduce the emission of the gases which result in acid rain)

Task

Carry out a survey in your class/year. Who would consider buying products that they knew were less harmful to the environment? Use diagrams/charts to show your survey's findings.

Marketing, Design and the Environment

Packaging: a case study

How can *you* help to protect the environment? Let's look at one example: packaging. Almost everything we buy today is packaged in some way, using materials such as paper, metal, glass and plastics.

Packaging has played an important part in the way we have lived over the last 20 to 30 years. For example, without the many different forms of packaging available now, there would not be as much choice on the food shelves in supermarkets. Packaging has also enabled products, especially foodstuffs, to be used straight off the shelf. Packaging is essential: it protects and assists the distribution and display of a product.

Over-packaging

Some products use more materials than is necessary. This is called over-packaging. It not only wastes packaging material but more energy is used to make the material in the first place. Below are some examples of over-packaging. These also trick consumers into thinking that they are getting more goods than they really are. What do you think about this?

Although these are examples of over-packaging, some containers are made to a standard size or sizes. This means that certain products, such as pills, are packaged in containers that are the nearest suitable size available and not the ideal size needed for the products.

False skin and/or bottom

Half-filled container

Half-filled package

Task

Have a look at various kinds of packaging. Identify one good and one bad example of packaging. Explain in a few sentences the reasons for your choices. Now redesign the bad example. Can any of the packages you looked at be used for anything else?

Fact File

Sixty per cent of all packaging used is for food.

Marketing and the Environment

Recycling

Recycling is the name given to the breaking down of used and waste material, such as newspapers, bottles and cartons, to make new materials like paper, glass and metal. However, recycling waste material is only worthwhile when less energy is used in the process than would be used in making new material from the beginning.

Paper

A lot of the paper we use can be recycled. Newspapers, magazines and boxes can be turned back into pulp and made into new paper. Recycling paper saves trees, uses fewer chemicals and up to 40 per cent less energy than making new paper.

Metal

Producing any type of metal uses a lot of energy, and one metal called aluminium uses up more than others. Many soft-drink cans are made from aluminium.

Other types of food cans are made from steel, which is covered in a layer of tin. You can tell whether a can is made from steel or aluminium by using a magnet. Aluminium will not be attracted to the magnet. Recycling aluminium cans saves up to 90 per cent of the energy used to make new cans.

Plastic

Plastic materials can also be recycled. There are many different types of plastic material and these can be difficult to separate in order to make new material.

Industry recycles about 30 per cent of its waste material. When William made his key fobs, he used a plastic called polythene. Some polythene waste can be recycled and, therefore, injection-moulded several times, although it is only a low percentage.

Fact File

Between two and three binloads of rubbish can produce the same heat energy as one bag of coal.

Task

Write down a list of the things you throw away in one day. List them under the headings Paper, Plastic, Metal and Glass. Can you reduce your daily wastage by only buying essential products, or by finding another use for their packaging?

Reusing

Reusing packaging such as glass containers saves more energy than recycling the same bottle after only one use. However, bottles made for recycling have to be stronger and heavier and more energy is needed to make them. Also, they have to be collected and this must be organized. The best example of the reuse of bottles in this country is the milk bottle.

In many European countries, notably Germany, the return (to the shop) of soft-drink containers made from certain plastic materials is compulsory!

There is no such thing as the perfect green product. No matter what materials or processes are used to make a product (or provide a service), it will do some harm to the environment. However, marketing and design can play an important role in reducing the harm to the environment. It will not be easy, but clever marketing and designing can:

1. Use materials that have been recycled.
2. Consider ways of reducing energy.
3. Reduce the amount of waste caused in the making of a product and in packaging it.
4. Design so that products can be reused.
5. Design a product so that it lasts longer, in other words, increase the life-cycle of a product.
6. Label packaging clearly. This will help educate the consumer about recycling and reusing materials as well as saving energy. In turn, this will reduce the harm to the environment.

Task

Design a label for a package which clearly shows that the material has been recycled or is suitable for recycling.

Fact File

To make one tonne of glass requires 12 tonnes of raw materials such as sand, soda and lime or just one tonne of recycled glass. This saves up to 30 gallons of fuel oil!

Mini-Dictionary

Acid rain Gases such as sulphur dioxide and carbon dioxide mix with water vapour to form a solution. This falls as acid rain.

Advertising A way of making known and promoting a product, e.g. through a poster.

Atmosphere Gases which surround the earth.

Average cost The cost of a single product, which is worked out by dividing the total costs by the number of products made.

Biodegradable A term used to describe materials which decompose or break up in the environment.

Business plan A plan of how much you intend to spend (cash outflow) and how much you expect to get back (cash inflow).

Competition Trying to do better than others.

Consumer/Customer The person who buys or uses products or services.

Consumer requirements The things which the buyer will want or expect from a product or service.

Costs The materials and services which have to be paid for by a business.

Distribution The ways and methods by which a product or service is delivered to a market.

Energy Power, e.g. electrical energy, which is needed to produce heat and light.

Environment The things around us, our surroundings. All the elements which affect how we live.

Fixed costs Costs that do not increase with output, e.g. rent, wages.

Forecast Looking into the future and planning, i.e. by making a business plan.

Fossil fuel A fuel, such as oil and gas, derived from the remains of plants and animals which died and decayed in early geological periods.

Green consumers The name given to consumers who buy products that are less harmful to the environment.

Green design The name given to products that have been designed in a way that makes them less harmful to the environment.

Greenhouse effect Gases such as carbon dioxide are produced when coal is burned. These gases rise up into the air and prevent the sun's heat from escaping harmlessly into space. Through this effect, the planet is warming up (global warming).

Incentive A reward (usually money) which is given to a company to encourage it to increase business, e.g. by establishing itself in an area of high unemployment.

Labour force People who are of working age with the skills/experience to carry out their job.

Legislation Laws passed by governments.

Manufacture To make or produce things.

Market A place where things are bought and sold. The people who will use or buy a product.

Market research The process of collecting information about markets and about the response to a product.

Marketing The process of identifying consumer needs and bringing consumers what they need at the right time and in the right place.

Marketing mix The ingredients of marketing: product, price, place, promotion.

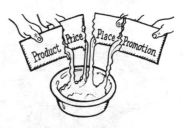

Nutritional value Nourishment value of food.

Ozone layer A layer of gas similar to oxygen that surrounds the earth.

Place Where a product is to be sold and how it is going to get there.

Price What something costs, plus the profit element. Price = total cost + profit element.

Mini-Dictionary

Product 1. Any item which is made or manufactured for sale or use. 2. The outcome of making or doing something.

Product life-cycle The length of time a product lasts.

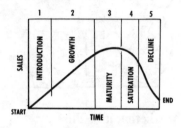

Production line The different stages needed to make a product.

Production run Producing a number of the same products continuously. The manufacturing process is kept running until the required number of products are made.

Profit That which is left after all the costs have been taken away.

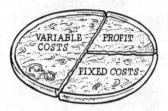

Profit element The amount of profit. Profit element = total cost − price.

Promotion Telling consumers about your product.

Raw materials Materials such as woods, metals and plastics which are used to make a product. These might be natural, such as wood, or manufactured, such as plastics.

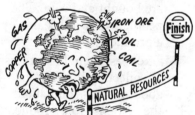

Recycling Breaking down waste materials, such as metal cans, so that the material can be used again.

Retail The sale of products, usually in a shop.

Retailer Someone who owns a retail outlet, i.e. a shop owner.

Reusing Using a product more than once before recycling.

Services Things which meet our needs or wants. Banks, schooling and transport are examples of service industries.

Unit cost The cost for a single item.

Variable costs Costs that can change as output increases, e.g. materials.

Warehouse A place where products are stored and sold, usually to retailers.

Wholesale The buying and selling of goods in large quantities from manufacturers. The manufacturer sells the goods at one price to the wholesaler, who then sells them at a higher price and in smaller quantities to a retailer. The retailer adds to the price (in order to make his or her profit) and sells the goods to customers.

Wholesaler A person who buys goods in bulk (large quantities) and sells them in smaller quantities to retailers.

Index

Acid rain 51
Advertising 9, 28–29
'Atmosphere 50
Average cost 46

Batch production 37
Bulk ordering 36
Business environment 32–33
Business plan 31

Cash inflow 31
Cash outflow 31
CFCs 51
Competition 46
Consumer 18
Consumer requirements 38–39
Consumer research 21
Corporate identity 15
Costs 9
Customer 18

Demand 19
Distribution 30
Desktop publishing 43

Economies of scale 46
Energy 50
Enterprise 47
Environment 48
European Community 17

Fixed costs 26, 46
Forecast 31
Fossil fuels 51

Government legislation 53
Green consumerism 52
Green consumers 52
Green design 54
Greenhouse effect 50

Incentives 32
Information design 42–45

Job production 37

Labour force 8, 32
Large-scale production 46
Legislation 32

Market research 20–23
Marketing 18–33
Marketing mix 24–30
Market-place 18
Mass production 37

Ozone layer 51

Packaging 34, 39–41, 55
Photocopying 12–13
Place 30
Price 26, 27
Primary industries 7
Product life-cycle 24–25
Product research 22
Production line 6
Production run 34
Profit 9, 14, 27
Profit element 27, 31, 46

Questionnaires 10, 22–23

Raw materials 7, 32
Recycling 56
Retailer 30
Reusing 57
Rubber-stamp printing 11

Sales promotion 29
Secondary industries 7

Tertiary industries 7

Unit cost 12, 14

Variable costs 26

Wholesale 30
Wholesaler 30